SLIP STREAM

CRAZY FOODS

ANNE ROONEY

EDGE
W
FRANKLIN WATTS

LONDON·SYDNEY

D0996055

Disclaimer – In the preparation of this book, all due care has been exercised with regard to the activities depicted. The Author and Publishers regret that they can accept no liability for any loss or injury sustained.

First published in 2014 by
Franklin Watts
338 Euston Road
London NW1 3BH

Franklin Watts Australia
Level 17/207 Kent Street
Sydney NSW 2000

© Franklin Watts 2013

(ebook) ISBN: 978 1 4451 2906 8
(pb) ISBN 978 1 4451 3228 0
(library ebook) ISBN: 978 1 4451 2508 4

Dewey Classification number: 641.3

A CIP catalogue record for this book is available from the British Library.

Series Editors: Adrian Cole and Jackie Hamley
Series Advisors: Diana Bentley and Dee Reid
Series Designer: Peter Scoulding

Printed in China

Franklin Watts is a division of Hachette Children's Books, an Hachette UK company.
www.hachette.co.uk

Acknowledgements:
Carmentianya/Dreamstime: 10.
Chrispyphoto/Dreamstime: 22.
CoolR/Shutterstock: 6.
Nikki Coulombe: 15.
dimitris-k/Shutterstock: 8.
Mark & Jana Faus/http://angolarising. blogspot.co.uk: 20.
Foodpictures/Shutterstock: 9t.
Christian Handl./Superstock: 17.
heinteh5/Shutterstock: 11.
Ulet Ifansasti/Getty Images: 19.
Emmanuel R Lacoste/Shutterstock: 4.
Lebrecht Music & Arts PL/Alamy: 13.
Jason Mintzer/Shutterstock: 14.
p.studio 66/Shutterstock: front cover.
Catalin Petolea/Shutterstock: 9b.
RGB Ventures LLC dba SuperStock/Alamy: 16.
Neil Setchfield/Alamy: 5.
Splosh/Dreamstime: 1, 23.
Taiftin/Shutterstock: 21.
Yasuko Takemoto/istockphoto: 7.
Sonny Tumbelaka/AFP/Getty Images: 18.
wikimedia: 12.

Every attempt has been made to clear copyright. Should there be any inadvertent omission please apply to the publisher for rectification.

CONTENTS

CAN YOU EAT IT?

People around the world eat lots of different things. Food that looks odd to us could be quite ordinary to someone else.

A restaurant near Oxford, UK, sells snail porridge.

ICE CREAM

What's your favourite ice cream?
Here are some flavours you might
not know. They're all real!
Would you like to try:

Bacon?
Cheese and spaghetti?
Squid ink?
Sardine and brandy?
Raw horse?
Pig's blood and chocolate?
Or octopus?

NETTLE SOUP

Stinging nettles can be painful. Have you ever been stung? But they don't sting when cooked and can taste quite nice! Some people make a soup out of nettles.

They have to wear rubber gloves to handle the nettles!

BIRD SPIT SOUP

Bird's nest soup is made from boiled bird nests. The nests are built by swallows that live in caves in China.

The swallow makes its nest from spit, which goes hard. Then people boil the nests.

ROMAN MEALS

Rich people in ancient Rome ate huge feasts. One special meal was a whole piglet stuffed with chicken, thrushes, sausages, snails and vegetables.

Rich Romans liked to eat peacock tongues. They also ate mice dipped in honey.

FRIED SNAKE

In parts of the USA people eat deep-fried rattlesnake.

The snake is cut into small chunks. Then it's dipped in batter and fried in hot oil. It's sometimes served with cactus.

STINKY FISH HEADS

To make 'stinkhead', Inuit cooks
cut the head off a large fish,
wrap it in grass and bury it.

After a few weeks, it's ready to eat — but it smells pretty bad!

SMELLY COFFEE

The most expensive coffee in the world is called 'kopi luwak'. It's made from coffee beans found in the dung of a civet cat.

The civet eats the beans, but can't digest them. The beans come out in its poo.

EATING BUGS

In Botswana, spiky caterpillars make a tasty soup. In Thailand, crickets, beetles, cockroaches and even scorpions are eaten!

FOOD ON A STICK

You might be used to lollipops on a stick. In China, people buy starfish, scorpions and seahorses on sticks. They make a crunchy snack.

Would you like to try one?
What other food would you like to taste?

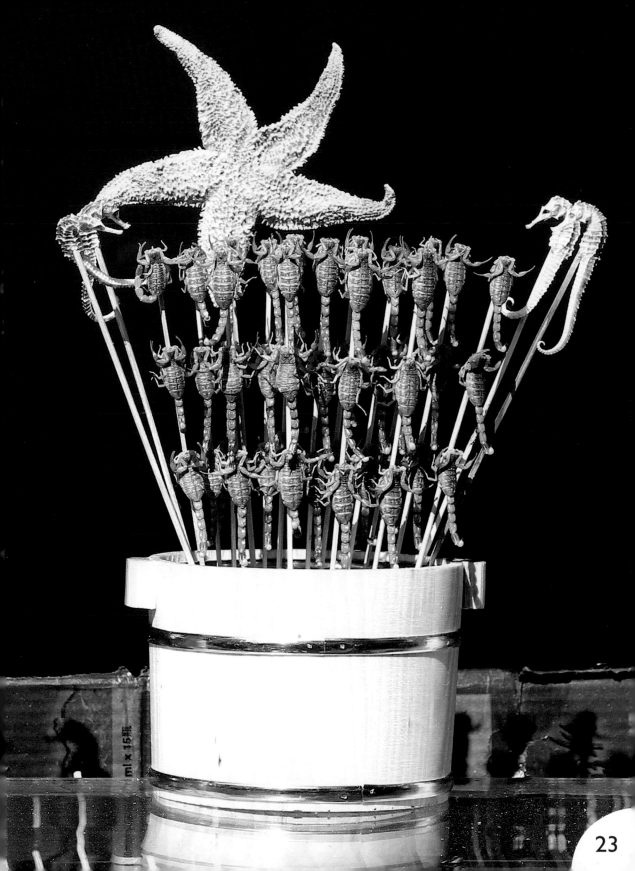

INDEX

About SLIPSTREAM

Slipstream is a series of expertly levelled books designed for pupils who are struggling with reading. Its unique three-strand approach through fiction, graphic fiction and non-fiction gives pupils a rich reading experience that will accelerate their progress and close the reading gap.

At the heart of every Slipstream non-fiction book is exciting information. Easily accessible words and phrases ensure that pupils both decode and comprehend, and the topics really engage older struggling readers.

Whether you're using Slipstream Level 2 for Guided Reading or as an independent read, here are some suggestions:

1. Make each reading session successful. Talk about the text before the pupil starts reading. Introduce any unfamiliar vocabulary.

2. Encourage the pupil to talk about the book using a range of open questions. For example, what is the worst or best food they can think of?

3. Discuss the differences between reading non-fiction, fiction and graphic fiction. Which do they prefer?

For guidance, SLIPSTREAM Level 2 – Crazy Food has been approximately measured to:

National Curriculum Level: 2b
Reading Age: 7.6–8.0
Book Band: Purple

ATOS: 2.5
Guided Reading Level: I
Lexile® Measure (confirmed): 630L

Slipstream Le
photocopiab
WORKBOOK
ISBN: 978 1 4451 1797 3
available – downloa
free sample
worksheets from:
www.franklinwatts.co.uk